E242
EDUCATION: A SECOND-LEVEL C

LEARNING FOR ALL

UNIT 16
LEARNING FOR ALL

Prepared for the course team by
Felicity Armstrong and Tony Booth

The Open University

E242 COURSE READERS

There are two course readers associated with E242; they are:

BOOTH, T., SWANN, W., MASTERTON, M. and POTTS, P. (eds) (1992) *Learning for All 1: curricula for diversity in education*, London, Routledge (**Reader 1**).

BOOTH, T., SWANN, W., MASTERTON, M. and POTTS, P. (eds) (1992) *Learning for All 2: policies for diversity in education*, London, Routledge (**Reader 2**).

TELEVISION PROGRAMMES AND AUDIO-CASSETTES

There are eight TV programmes and three audio-cassettes associated with E242. They are closely integrated into the unit texts and there are no separate TV or cassette notes. However, you may obtain further information about them by writing to Open University Educational Enterprises Ltd, 12 Cofferidge Close, Stony Stratford, Milton Keynes MK11 1BY.

Cover illustration shows a detail from 'Midsummer Common' by Dorothy Bordass.

The Open University, Walton Hall, Milton Keynes MK7 6AA

First published 1993

Copyright © 1993 The Open University

All rights reserved. No part of this publication may be reproduced, stored in a retrieval system or transmitted, in any form or by any means, without written permission from the publisher or a licence from the Copyright Licensing Agency Limited. Details of such licences (for reprographic reproduction) may be obtained from the Copyright Licensing Agency Ltd, 90 Tottenham Court Road, London W1P 9HE.

Edited, designed and typeset by The Open University.

Printed in Scotland by Thomson Litho Ltd, East Kilbride.

ISBN 0 7492 3115 7

This unit forms part of an Open University course; the complete list of units is printed at the end of this book. If you have not enrolled on the course and would like to buy this or other Open University material, please write to Open University Educational Enterprises Ltd, 12 Cofferidge Close, Stony Stratford MK11 1BY, United Kingdom. If you wish to enquire about enrolling as an Open University student, please write to the Admissions Office, The Open University, PO Box 48, Walton Hall, Milton Keynes MK7 6AB, United Kingdom.

1.1

e242u16i1.1

CONTENTS

1	**Introduction**	4
	How to study this unit	5
2	**Responding to difference at Hirst High**	6
	Background to a developing school	6
	Hirst High: a comprehensive community school	7
	The closure of Riverbank Special School	11
	The model of integration	12
	Groups and timetables: constraints on participation	14
	Setting for 'learning support'	16
	Sets for units of accreditation	17
	Setting by gender	17
	Staff sets	18
	Students' views of setting	18
	The timetable: from six days to ten	19
	From Riverbank school to the special needs department	20
	Participation in lessons	22
	Informal contact between students	24
	Physical access	28
	Contact between staff	29
	The attitude of students	29
	The views of parents	30
	A new role for the special needs department?	31
	Including some, excluding others?	31
	Conclusion: raising questions	32
3	**Controlling change**	33
	Picking up the 1992 Education Bill	34
	Formal school plans	36
	Perspectives from special schools	38
4	**A common concern**	46
	Concluding remarks	49
	References	51
	Acknowledgements	51

1 INTRODUCTION

1.1 The last unit of a course can be made to carry too heavy a burden. At the end of a course, authors may be tempted to cram in the latest information from schools and government in an effort to stop the course going out of date. However, we do not wish to overload you or tie the course to a particular period of time. Instead, in this final unit we will provide a number of opportunities to reflect on the concerns of the course.

1.2 After exploring the power of Nottinghamshire LEA to co-ordinate educational change in Unit 15, Patricia Potts and Will Swann urged us to be cautious about attributing an LEA's difficulties in implementing policy to particular education laws: 'An LEA's capacity to affect what happens in schools has always been limited. The question now is: how much more has it been limited by the Reform Act?' (Unit 15, p. 36). When we were writing this unit, local government control of education was being further weakened by new legislation in the form of an education bill for England and Wales, which was working its way through the committee stages of the House of Commons. This had the major purposes of encouraging more schools to opt out of local democratic control and of providing an alternative system for financing and rationalizing them. The bill followed a White Paper called *Choice and Diversity* (DfE, 1992), which was released in the summer of 1992 with a consultation period until mid-September of that year, by which time, so we were reliably informed, the bill had already been printed. We will provide a brief summary of the bill and its implications for students who experience difficulties or who have disabilities.

1.3 The 1993 Education Act is only one of many influences that will affect education during the life of this course. The effect of such external influences depends on the way they are absorbed by practitioners. It is one of the aims of this course to extend *your* influence on education by encouraging you to link ideas about practice to a firm set of principles. We do not want you to see a law in education as though it was part of a training manual for magistrates, but as requirements to be fitted in to your own considered view of how teaching and learning should take place. The more you influence education, the less it will depend on other forces.

1.4 The three main sections of this unit perform different tasks and you should be prepared for shifts of focus as you move from one to the other. Section 2 of this unit, 'Responding to difference at Hirst High', is a detailed case study of the way one comprehensive school divided and categorized its students according to their attainment and assumptions about their ability. We examined the school at the point when it had just included a group of students categorized as having severe learning difficulties. To what extent can a comprehensive school provide a learning environment in which all students participate and are positively valued irrespective of their level of attainment or disability? How do the new students fit into the pre-existing culture and structure of the school? Our case study provides an opportunity to reflect on the effects of grouping and setting policies. It is also a reminder of the complexity of schools and the need to avoid glib generalizations about the way they operate.

1.5   In Section 3, 'Controlling change', we survey, briefly, new pressures on education, particularly those proposed in the 1992 Education Bill. We examine the scope for those working in mainstream and special schools and colleges to take control of their own policies. We consider the scope for formal school development plans to enable staff in schools to absorb official pressures into their own values and approaches to education. We will consider the perspective of those working within special schools and look at two examples of special schools that have deliberately changed their roles.

1.6   The final section of the unit, 'A common concern', asks you to reflect on the principles underlying the course and their practical implications. Unless you stumbled into the course by accident you will share with other course participants, and with ourselves, concerns for students who experience difficulties in education and for disabled students. Students may experience difficulties either in interpreting the curriculum or may bring their vulnerabilities to school or be made vulnerable once they are there. In what ways do our concerns limit the range of principles and practices that we should adopt in education?

HOW TO STUDY THIS UNIT

1.7   This unit should take up two weeks study time. Section 2 is by far the longest part of the unit but Section 3, which includes three chapters from Reader 2, involves more reading overall. Listed below is the material other than this text that you will study in each section, and where it can be found.

Section 2 Responding to difference at Hirst High

Cassette 2, Programme 4: *Responding to Difference.*

Section 3 Controlling change

Reader 2, Chapter 3: 'Planning school development', by Christine Gilbert.

Reader 2, Chapter 4: 'Finding a new place: changes in role at Ormerod Special School' by Tim Southgate.

Reader 2, Chapter 5: 'Moving in and moving out: the closure of Etton Pasture Special School' by Roger Kidd.

Section 4 A common concern

No additional material.

2 RESPONDING TO DIFFERENCE AT HIRST HIGH

BACKGROUND TO A DEVELOPING SCHOOL

2.1 To understand how difficulties in learning arise in a particular school we need to look at the organization and curriculum of the whole school. For example, the way schools group students as good or less good learners has consequences for how they are taught and how they are valued by teachers, other students and themselves. If we assign different groups of students a different value based on their attainment we are devaluing some students relative to others. Devaluation may lead to disaffection which in turn is likely to interfere with learning. Disaffection and difficulties in learning may also be seen as reasons for excluding students from a central place in the curricula of a school or from the school itself. The exclusion of students from a school can be seen, then, as only one aspect of the categorization and selection processes operating within all schools. These processes are best understood by looking carefully at particular schools and that is what we have started to do at Hirst High, a school in Ashington, Northumberland.

2.2 We chose to examine Hirst High because in October 1991 the school included a group of students categorized as having 'severe learning difficulties' in a newly adapted area of the school called the 'special needs department'. They joined the school when their special school closed, with the middle school group joining the adjacent Seaton Hirst Middle School. A few years earlier the first school group from the special school had joined Abbeyfield First School, a mainstream school in Morpeth.

2.3 The new students are very varied in their interests and attainments but include some students with little evidence of understanding of language or capacity for voluntary movement. Such students are commonly seen as being among the most difficult to include within the mainstream, particularly after primary age. If they can participate in a comprehensive secondary education what reason is there for excluding other students who may experience less severe difficulties?

2.4 The presence of this group of categorized students within the school helps to reveal, as well as call into question, the way all students are classified and assigned values as learners. Systems for dividing students into groups by attainment impose constraints on the participation of students viewed as having learning difficulties. Equally, pressure for greater participation of students categorized as having learning difficulties challenges these systems and reveals the strength of commitment to them. Asking questions about grouping and categorization policies is one way to approach the process of integration. Examining the progress of and barriers to integration helps to reveal the categorization processes operating in a school.

2.5   This section describes a developing school in the early stages of the inclusion of a new group of students. We start by examining, briefly, the ethos and structure of the High School since it opened, the background to the closure of Riverbank Special School and the approach to integration. We then introduce the cassette programme which concentrates on the first half of our story of the school, the way the school divided students by attainment and presumed ability and structured its time before it was joined by students from Riverbank Special School. We then take up the story of the inclusion of the new group of students and staff at the school.

Hirst High: a comprehensive community school

2.6   Hirst High School has about 800 students aged 13 to 18 years (year 9 onwards) and was purpose-built as a mixed comprehensive school, opening in 1974, on the edge of a large housing estate in North Seaton, Ashington, about twenty miles north of Newcastle. It was formed from an amalgamation of secondary modern schools which had become co-educational a year earlier. Its wide playing fields extend to the rows of terraced houses which make up the estate. In the distance to the east lies Newbiggin-by-the-Sea and to the north along the coast the power station at Lyme Sands. To the south-east lies the disused North Seaton Colliery and industrial estate. This was once a thriving mining and fishing community but now only one pit remains open in the area – at Ellington – and the fishing boats at Newbiggin are reduced to a tiny fleet. ALCAN, the aluminium smelter, was the main provider of employment in this area but has laid off large numbers of workers.

2.7   The Woodhorn Colliery Museum provides a vivid introduction to the history of the local mining community. The lives of generations of local miners and their families are illustrated by a collection of paintings by the Ashington Group, a group of miners some of whom started painting together at a Workers Education Association class in the 1930s.

2.8   Richard Houlden was appointed as the head teacher when the school opened and has remained since. He explained to us how the school, in its early days, sought to divorce its comprehensive culture from any roots within the secondary modern schools from which it had emerged. The staff wanted the school to be 'achievement oriented' and this is reflected in the 'hall of fame' in the entrance area to the school, where there are photographs and descriptions of students who have gone on to university. The staff devised a system of mixed attainment tutor groups from which students were assigned to multiple sets for a variety

7

Pit ponies with Ashington Colliery in the background. Untitled painting by Oliver Kilbourne of the Ashington Group (1959).

Ashington was once a thriving mining community, but most of the pits in the area have now closed down.

Woodhorn Colliery closed in 1981 and is now a museum.

of subjects based on their attainments. The setting system of the first year students (year 9) gave way to option choices in the 14+ curriculum, as Richard Houlden explained:

> You began to achieve a sort of setting by choice... On the whole it's the relatively able youngsters who did O-level physics, not the least able and so on, so it began to sort itself out. So those traditions have been followed on through and they've been very important to us.

2.9   However, in a number of ways the school attempted to adopt a broad concept of achievement. In particular, there was very strong encouragement to students to stay on in the sixth form. Richard Houlden said:

> We were saying to people with two O levels from a very early stage, you can come in the sixth form, the only criteria is that we want to know and understand that the course you want to do makes sense and makes sense for you in educational terms and it provides you with worthwhile targets ...

> In the sixth altogether, we have a staying-on rate of about 40 per cent, which from this sort of area is a very high figure indeed. Only about a third of our sixth-formers are really academic in the sense that they're the people for whom A level is intended as an appropriate target ... The point I'm making is that over the years we've had to adapt and we have had to look at the ways in which we receive different groups and the way they fit in.

2.10   The way the learning difficulties of students were identified and supported underwent a series of changes which were similar to those described in Units 1/2 and 6/7. Gwen Woodman, the co-ordinator for learning support and a member of the senior management team in the school, described developments in learning support from the mid-eighties:

> ... about five or six years ago these special needs students in mainstream were part of what you would call the remedial provision where most of their time was spent with one or two teachers, very limited curriculum, very limited access to facilities. About five years ago we embarked upon a very large programme of staff in-service. Out of this came a change in provision so that all of the youngsters had total access to the curriculum and to all areas of the school and consequently access to all staff.

2.11   In practice, this meant that instead of being in a remedial class and receiving a different curriculum, the students with the lowest attainments became the lowest set, but that any teacher might be timetabled to teach them. Initially these students were offered in-class support, but Gwen Woodman argued that the setting system and the increase in contact and confidence between teachers and these students enabled this to be reduced:

> Teachers have become more confident with the youngsters and therefore the level of support has in a sense been withdrawn – by that I mean direct support in the classroom. Staff can come at any time to talk to me about various issues relating to worksheets, teaching methods, specifically about youngsters – I still do a lot of that – but on the whole staff have moved on a long way and are able to cope very much with the special needs youngsters themselves and that's the stage we're at. There's no special department but there is somebody there to support staff and students and to make sure they get full access to the curriculum.

Gwen Woodman still operates a system of withdrawal to teach some students basic English, during four out of six modern language lessons.

2.12   Hirst High School has strong links with the local community. The buildings and facilities are available to local people to pursue educational and leisure activities. The library is shared by the school and the local community. School dinner times are also shared by local people, especially those who have retired, who may wish to come and have a meal alongside pupils and staff. It is a friendly and welcoming school. The role of local community life and attitudes is acknowledged and celebrated at Hirst High School but concern is also voiced about the future of local young people now that the traditional industries have virtually gone and unemployment is endemic in the area.

A school for a community.

2.13   Unemployment in the area is only one indication of the economic pressures affecting the school. The cuts to the local authority budget in the early 1990s had put a large number of community education projects at risk and pushed class size up and reduced the planning periods for teachers.

The closure of Riverbank Special School

2.14   In the early 1980s, Riverbank was a school for pupils of all ages who were described as having 'severe or profound learning difficulties'. The school occupied two sites – one on a run-down industrial estate in North Seaton for the younger pupils and the other in Newbiggin for students of secondary age. The buildings were outdated and in need of improvement and the pressure on existing accommodation was increasing. The long-term plans of the county council included a new purpose-built school on a greenfield site to replace the existing buildings when funds 'became available'. However, the pressing need to accommodate more children meant that there was not time to wait for funding and during 1984–5 children of first school age moved from the North Seaton annexe to occupy spare accommodation on the same site as Abbeyfield First School in Morpeth.

2.15   At the time, according to a local education officer, parents of both mainstream children and of those coming from Riverbank were wary of the change. How would mainstream children react to these children, some of whom had profound disabilities, being educated at their school? Would the presence of these children hold back the learning of mainstream children? Would the children from Riverbank have the specialist help and accommodation which they needed? However, in time, parents and teachers of both the mainstream school and the Riverbank annexe began to appreciate that there were positive advantages of the groups being together and an increasing number of shared activities took place. In 1988, some modest adaptations were made to Abbeyfield and instead of remaining as an annexe of Riverbank the children described as having severe learning difficulties were included on the Abbeyfield roll. The successful experience at Abbeyfield was a major factor in the decision not to build a new special school. The local education authority decided to extend the Abbeyfield project through similar amalgamations of the Riverbank school with a middle and high school.

2.16   When the pupils and staff at the Newbiggin annexe of Riverbank school moved to Hirst High in October 1991, those at the Riverbank base at North Seaton moved to Seaton Hirst Middle School which has a site adjoining Hirst High School. Major adaptations had been made to both schools with purpose-built suites including rooms for speech therapy and physiotherapy and, at the middle school, a hydrotherapy pool.

2.17   Before they joined the school, the staff at Riverbank had been developing their own approach to the grouping and timetabling of their students. In some respects their grouping policies had been moving away from those they would meet at Hirst High. Before April 1991, their groups were divided according to 'ability', with the special care group taught separately. This change will be familiar to you from reading Jenny Corbett's study for Unit 8/9 (Reader 1, Chapter 17). Subsequently students were organized in classes of about six students grouped according to age, but with their own teacher and teaching assistant for the whole day.

2.18   There had been increasing contact with other high school students and staff prior to the move. Initially this was with Ashington High and then with Hirst High. Students visited Hirst High for a variety of lessons in craft, science and technology, and students were introduced to each other in leisure activities.

The model of integration

2.19   As you will be aware from the discussions in Unit 1/2 and elsewhere in the course, there are a variety of models for integration. Some people think of integration as the insertion of 'special students' and their support into an otherwise unchanged mainstream institution. We think of integration as linked to a process of developing mainstream, comprehensive, nursery, primary, secondary and further education so that devaluations are reduced and participation for all is enhanced. It involves examining curricula, organization, teaching and learning methods to encourage these developments.

2.20   Schools that are more willing and able to respond to a diversity of background and attainment in students are more likely to include students in their communities with limited development of language or with disabilities. For Chris Raine (Reader 1, Chapter 12), who had never been excluded from the mainstream, support was brought into the school in his community and the whole school adapted in order to provide a responsive place for his learning. But often when students are moved from special schools, they are grouped together in a mainstream school which may be some distance from their homes. Later in the unit Tim Southgate explains how, for some disabled students who had attended the special school of which he was head, the model changed over time from a grouping by category to providing support in a local school. This shift can be related to the view of integration promoted in this course as a never-ending process of increasing participation. It can also be seen as part of a new emphasis on the categorization by presumed ability of disabled students and those who experience difficulties in learning. Students who are categorized as low in attainment are more likely to be excluded from the mainstream than other students, irrespective of disability, and are less likely to be supported back into the mainstream once they have attended special schools. When they do move back in, they are more likely to be grouped together in a specially resourced mainstream school than included in their local school.

2.21   However, the model of local inclusion *has* been attempted with students categorized as having severe learning difficulties by Ken Jupp, the head of Overdale Special School in Stockport for primary-aged students. He was instrumental in establishing a pilot scheme whereby five students chosen randomly from his school attended their local primary school. Each child was supported by a full-time learning support assistant. A peripatetic specialist teacher provided teaching support to all five schools. Despite the apparent success of the project, when the local authority planned to extend the project, it opted (to the disappointment of Ken Jupp) for a system of resourced schools where five or six students from Overdale would be grouped in one school. These children, however, would be supported within mainstream classes (Jupp, 1992).

2.22   In the case of Riverbank, the previous movement of a group of children to Abbeyfield First School may have helped to narrow the choices about what approach to adopt. The decision to dissolve Riverbank into three departments with staff and students attached to mainstream schools was different too from the model at Bishopswood, a 'severe learning difficulties school' in South Oxfordshire. All the students and staff at Bishopswood moved from their special school base into classes in a nursery, primary and comprehensive school. However, they remained members of Bishopswood, which continued as a special school with its own head, governing body and funding (CSIE, 1992). The Bishopswood staff meet 'at least once a week' and 'pupils and staff come together twice a term for assemblies and social events, which are times of celebration' (CSIE, 1992, p. 3). The Bishopswood staff argue that a separate identity enables them to acquire funds additional to their capitation allowances:

> Our capitation is boosted by donations and funds raised by the school association (BSA); this extra financial support is essential and could not be guaranteed if our children were on the roll of mainstream schools.

> It is usually only when fund-raising that the phrase 'special school for handicapped children' may be used. This is an unfortunate necessity which continues to cause embarrassment, though parents say staff can be too sensitive in their wish to avoid labels. When we became fully based in partner schools, Bishopswood held a wine

and cheese evening to explain to parents and teachers in partner schools why some separate fund raising would remain essential.

(CSIE, 1992, p. 12)

2.23   Unit 14 provided the views and feelings of disabled people about their portrayal as charity cases. Many feel that money raised through such means is no compensation for the assault on their human dignity and obscures the need to campaign for rights and respect.

2.24   You will have further opportunities to reflect on models of integration in Section 3 of this unit. It may help you in weighing up alternatives to approach them from the point of view of the students. To what extent is it in the interests of students who experience difficulties or who have disabilities to be grouped together at school or college? Deaf students' need for a signing community may make it hard to envisage their education in local schools, but what of students like those from Riverbank school whose language attainment and physical skills may be relatively limited for their age?

GROUPS AND TIMETABLES: CONSTRAINTS ON PARTICIPATION

Cassette 2, Programme 4, is called *Responding to Difference*. It introduces you to some of the teachers and students at Hirst High. They describe the way students are categorized by attainment within the school and the consequences this has for the gender composition of groups. They discuss the school timetable and the reasons for it. The programme begins to raise questions about how the students who had recently arrived from Riverbank Special School might participate in the school. At the time of making the programme the arrival of the students created a very early categorization problem. Within the school a group of students, placed in a bottom set on entry to the school, were already spoken of as having 'special needs' and the teacher with responsibility for them, Gwen Woodman, was the 'co-ordinator for special needs'. The students and staff from Riverbank were based in a new 'department of special needs' in Hirst High and their head of department, Eileen Farnham, who had previously been head of the senior Riverbank department, was described as the head of the special needs department. Gwen Woodman was given responsibility for ensuring smooth communication between school management and the new department. She subsequently relabelled her activities as 'learning support'. As you attempt to understand our description of the school you have to be aware of the ways in which the term 'special needs' was used in the school and the roles of various members of staff.

The programme opens with an extract from a GCSE lesson in which students were asked to prepare a short improvisation on the situations in which it would be appropriate to use standard English and those where it would be appropriate to use the dialect of the North-east. We used this sequence to provoke thought about the subtle ways in which students may be categorized in schools and the value that may attach to them as a result.

When we examined the grouping policies we encountered an unexpected result. The setting policies of the school produced large gender differences in the composition of groups. We were forced again to confront the important area of gender differences in performance and categorization, discussed in Unit 11/12 in relation to students categorized as having difficulties in behaviour.

Activity 1   Responding to difference

Listen to Cassette 2, Programme 4, now.

As you listen to the programme, think about the following questions:

- What effects do the grouping policies have on the way students learn and the difficulties they encounter?

- In particular, what effects do the grouping policies have on the way school achievement is perceived by boys and girls?

- What effects do pre-existing grouping policies have for the inclusion of students categorized as having 'severe learning difficulties' within the school?

2.25   In responding to the cassette programme, we have concentrated on the second half of the story about the inclusion of students from Riverbank school, which is only barely introduced in the programme. However, we have also added a number of comments on the grouping and timetabling arrangements for the whole school and reinforced others. The opening sequence to the programme, a mock interview with the Newcastle United manager, was recorded when the team were close to the bottom of the second division of the football league. When we were writing this, in December 1992, Newcastle led their division and were very likely to join the premier league in 1993. Perhaps this would have affected the way the manager was portrayed. The lesson had been set up to illustrate the way that different dialects might be appropriate for different audiences but it was clear that it raised questions about the accents and forms of expression that would be valued within schools and the effects this might have on students' readiness and capacities for learning.

2.26   Hirst High School provides a contrast to Whitmore High School's mixed-attainment grouping policy, which is described in Unit 1/2 (pp. 71–9) and in the reading on development plans (Reader 2, Chapter 3) which you will read later in this unit. It is the system at Whitmore school which is the more unusual. Dividing students into different groupings according to attainment and perceived ability is commonplace at secondary schools. The way it is done varies between schools and within subject areas, but there are very few schools where there is no streaming or setting of any kind. In Northumberland, according to one local authority officer, students are set in some way at all high schools, and some middle schools adopt a system of setting from the age of nine. At Hirst High the head linked the policy of setting to a desire for the school to be, and to be seen as, achievement oriented. The majority of pupils in the school (but not those who were part of the special needs department) belonged to mixed-attainment tutor groups and spent the last period each day with their tutor. But for nearly every part of the curriculum there was some sort of setting system, either as a result of a policy decision taken by the department or as a result of setting in other subjects which had produced constraints on the timetable.

2.27   In the programme, four main reasons were given for setting:

- It is easier to give pupils the kinds of courses they need; these different courses are designed to respond to differences in perceived ability.

- Mixed-attainment teaching 'holds the brighter ones back'.

- It is easier to teach groups of pupils who are divided up according to attainment.

- Setting makes it possible to meet the needs of all pupils.

2.28   Although in theory students could have been in different sets for different subjects, most departments followed the setting decisions made by the maths and English departments. The French department, for example, allocated students to its sets on the basis of the sets they were in for English. The science department has a rather different system; in that there is a set 1 and a set 2 and then the rest of the pupils are divided into what are referred to as 'mixed-ability sets'. But in what sense were these 'mixed ability' if the pupils who were seen as the highest attainers in science were extracted?

2.29   A further hidden anomaly is that although in theory pupils were able to move between sets – and in practice some did – the fact that the setting system was designed to offer different teaching both in content and delivery to different pupils meant that a pupil who was moved 'up' a set found themselves at a disadvantage in having to make up ground.

Setting for 'learning support'

2.30   Students were allocated to sets when they arrived at the school in year 9. Pupils who found themselves in set 5 for English arrived there by a rather different route from that of other students. Gwen Woodman, who was the co-ordinator for 'learning support', made sure that students she identified as needing learning support at their middle schools were placed in set 5 for English. Since modern language sets are based on English sets, she could withdraw them from modern languages for four of their lessons and give them help with their English to 'get their skills boosted up ... in the year 9'. There were a number of implications of this policy. It was harder for pupils to move to a higher set once they had arrived at the school with a 'special needs' label. Withdrawal from French on a regular basis made it very difficult for them to cover the same amount of ground in French as their peers and may have limited their future option choices.

2.31   Besides withdrawing students in year 9 for additional English, Gwen Woodman taught the lower-attaining option groups in year 10 and 11 for English lessons.

Sets for units of accreditation

2.32   For years 10 and 11, students were divided, for any particular subject, between GCSE and units of accreditation groups. The latter course consisted of short modules which were individually assessed and recorded on a certificate. A young English teacher explained what units of accreditation had to offer. Her previous teaching experience had been in a school where there had been banding, that is students were divided into broad streams according to 'presumed ability':

> You'd only get two groups which were designated an 'upper' one and a 'lower' one. I prefer setting because we do the units of accreditation. There was nothing like that so the ones at the bottom ended up with nothing. The most important thing is that the ones in the bottom set have something to work for, so when they leave some of them have piles of certificates saying exactly what they have done. One of the problems with those groups is truancy, so if you've got some who don't come to school regularly they can much more easily pick it up when they come back and it doesn't matter if they are not doing the same as everybody else.

Setting by gender

2.33   The most striking unplanned consequence of the setting system was the overwhelming predominance of girls in 'top' sets and boys in 'bottom' sets. Only in set 3 did there appear to be a fairly consistent balance between the two. This led too to an imbalance of the sexes in PE and games groups, because these were timetabled against languages.

One by-product of the setting system was the overwhelming preponderance of girls in top sets ...   *... and boys in lower sets.*

17

2.34   The school staff were well aware of the unequal achievement of girls and boys, the fact that boys were less positive about school than girls and of the need to do something about both of these issues. Some students and teachers suggested that boys were in lower sets because of their behaviour. Disruptive behaviour can itself be an expression of negative attitudes to what is being offered in school. It can also be an expression of feelings of hopelessness in an area and at a time when unemployment is very high. It could be that the setting system reinforced or produced, in part, differences in attainment and behaviour between groups. Should adjustments to the setting system be part of a strategy to raise the achievement of boys without interfering in the learning of girls?

Staff sets

2.35   At Hirst High, the head teacher and the three deputy heads were men. In common with a majority of secondary schools and most other institutions there are few women in senior management positions. One could argue that in the adult community there is a predominance of males in the 'top set'. How do students and staff make sense of this?

Students' views of setting

2.36   We asked neither staff or students about their views of staff sets, but we did ask students what they felt about student sets. The answers we obtained contradicted any presumption that students in lower sets would uniformly object to the system and their place within it. Hirst High seemed to go to considerable lengths to positively value the learning of students and we gained the impression that most students recognized this whatever set they were in. Of course, most had gone through middle schools where setting was accepted, particularly in the upper years, so they may not have had recent experience of mixed-attainment teaching groups.

2.37   There was general agreement that it was possible to move between sets which was clearly a motivating factor for some pupils. However, students also expressed doubts about whether a teacher would actually realize that a student was in the 'wrong' set.

2.38   Several of the students felt that the setting system led to the positive and negative labelling of pupils as 'brainy' or 'thick'. Some argued that students felt unhappy about themselves if they were moved from an upper to a lower set and that students from top and bottom sets did not mix much socially, which may have had particular effects on relationships between boys and girls.

2.39   On the cassette programme, Michael described a system in which pupils would not be divided up into different sets but would help each other learn in groups:

If you haven't got top sets and bottom sets, like, the not so brainy ones will learn off you and you'll learn more off the teacher so it's in a chain ... If one says 'Oh, what's ...?' and the brainy one says, 'Oh such and such ...' And it could be his friend who's not so brainy and he says, 'Why, the teacher didn't tell us that but *you* told us so we're one step forward!'

Activity 2　Arguments for setting

- How would you summarize the arguments for and against the setting system at Hirst High?

- To what extent might a setting system reinforce differences in achievement and behaviour?

- How might this be overcome?

- Could another system of grouping students in school serve the purpose of meeting the needs of all students more effectively?

The timetable: from six days to ten

2.40　In the programme, Bill Gould explained the particular local characteristics which he felt were important in deciding on the timetable. He had felt that only by having a six-day timetable could the school mitigate the problem of certain lessons being regularly missed by some pupils because of working patterns in the mines and market day.

2.41　There were a number of reasons given for changing from a six-day to a ten-day timetable. The 60 slots available over a ten-day cycle made it easier for the timetabler to respond to the intricate demands of the National Curriculum. The six-day timetable made it difficult to organize activities with agencies outside the school, such as regular joint sporting activities with other schools. It had posed particular difficulties in relation to visits from Riverbank school before its students transferred to Hirst High. One teacher argued that the school should go one step further and make the timetable conform to the real world of days of the week.

Activity 3　In the interests of the timetable

How do you respond to the arguments for a 60-period ten-day timetable? How far can a secondary timetable be simplified? How does it constrain the organization of the curriculum and the participation of students?

2.42　The arguments presented for the 60-period ten-day timetable are only partly concerned with the effective learning of students. Many teachers argue that students learn best with the minimum changes of teachers and subject matter. If this is so, then it is illogical to argue that the teaching of the national curriculum requires greater fragmentation of

19

student experience, for the effective teaching of the national curriculum, as of other curricula, must depend on the creation of good conditions for learning. If it is not realistic to build a timetable around the learning needs of students, what are schools for?

FROM RIVERBANK SCHOOL TO THE SPECIAL NEEDS DEPARTMENT

2.43   In October 1991, 29 students, six teachers, six teaching assistants, a full-time physiotherapist, and a speech therapist visiting one day a week became the new special needs department at Hirst High. This notion that the students and staff constituted a 'department', like other departments at the school such as maths or modern languages, may have made it seem natural, to many, that the students should spend most of their time there: maths teachers teach maths students and 'special needs' teachers teach 'special needs' students. Yet the special needs department, unlike any other department of the school, was expected to deliver the bulk of the curriculum to its students.

2.44   We have mentioned the confusion of terms that arose initially between mainstream and special 'special needs', which was eased, partly, by making one of Gwen Woodman's roles that of 'co-ordinator of learning support'. But there was another odd consequence of thinking of Riverbank students as transposed into the special needs department. Although they had joined a mainstream school, most staff referred to them as 'special needs students', differentiated from the rest of the students who were 'mainstream' students. It was as if the division between special-care and other students that used to exist at Riverbank Special School was being recreated within Hirst High, but now all the students from Riverbank were being assigned to the special category. The experience was rather like that at Springfield Road Junior School before the staff decided to amalgamate the severe learning difficulties unit with the rest of the school (Booth and Jones, 1987). When students from the unit there visited mainstream classes, they were known as 'special needs' or even 'units'. When they were on the class-register of mainstream classes they were referred to by their names. From the outside looking in on Hirst High, it seemed that the divisions might be broken down if the students from Riverbank could become members of the mixed-attainment tutor groups. However, it became apparent that this required a far greater change in thinking within the school than we had imagined and that if it were to happen at all it would take place only after gradually increasing contact of staff and students in a variety of other situations. As the head teacher observed:

> You have to move towards integration slowly. I don't think you can rush it. Attitudes have to change and develop. People need to have time to come to terms with it. Certainly in terms of the philosophy of the special needs department we believed they needed a secure base and they can get themselves established there and then they

can move out. But perhaps in concentrating on *them* needing a secure base, we also recognize that *we* needed them to have a secure base...

2.45   For some, the initial contacts emphasized differences in culture between the groups. Students and staff were on first-name terms in Riverbank, there was no uniform and there were fewer rules. One teacher described how she responded to being part of a larger, more complex and rule-governed organization after knowing the small, more relaxed community at Riverbank:

> They have obviously got to have rules which we didn't have to have in a smaller school. We had this small organization, this smaller sort of society where we didn't have to have so many rules. Now we've got to sort of 'police' our end of the corridor and do a break duty and I found it really difficult to say, 'What are you doing here? Should you be here? All right, but I'll have to check with your tutor.' I don't like doing it because I can't actually answer to myself why they should be outside and why they shouldn't lean on the radiator because it's lovely and warm [inside] and freezing outside. I know we're going to have to change, there's no doubt about it! Perhaps they'll have to change a little bit as well.

2.46   And there were other changes in structure to which staff had to adapt. The special needs department had been part of a special school, albeit on three sites, with its own identity and hierarchy. For Eileen Farnham, the head of the department, this involved less adaptation than, for example, the head of the middle-school department, who had been acting head of the special school. However, two members of the secondary department left, soon after the amalgamation, to work in special schools.

2.47   The special school staff had been used to a close relationship with the local authority who were still their employers. The rest of the school, used to devolved management, felt almost totally autonomous. The local management of special schools, promoted within the 1992 Education Bill, would presumably bring the sets of staff closer together in this respect. In 1992 they had separate as well as joint funds provided by the LEA. With local management, funding devolves to the school as a whole.

2.48   Eileen Farnham had expected that the school would develop a clear plan for increasing the participation of Riverbank students, which would then be implemented and supported. Instead she had to work with a more gradual policy involving increasing contact with staff and students but with no explicit agenda.

2.49   Three months after we made the recordings, the students in the special needs department appeared to have settled in and were enjoying life at Hirst High. Some could find their way around the school confidently and independently. Those who offered an opinion said they liked being at Hirst High. Reasons given were 'the uniform', 'more friends', 'better classrooms' and 'the dinners'.

2.50   Hirst High offered the students a wider range of activities than those available at Riverbank. How were the students to be given access to these? Clearly the students from Riverbank were not going to be integrated directly into the existing structures of tutor groups and sets. But the tutor groups and setting system and the 60-period, ten-day timetable were fixed points around which any participation had to be organized.

2.51   Meetings were held regularly when the team in the special needs department sat down together and considered each child individually to make sure that 'their needs were being met' and that there was a balance in the timetable. Although team members were keen to take advantage of what was on offer from the mainstream timetable and mainstream staff, as Eileen Farnham pointed out, they needed to look very closely at the content and teaching strategies of mainstream lessons. While opportunities for sharing lessons and staff were welcomed, some staff felt that their careful planning of the curriculum might be upset. As one teacher put it, 'We are in danger of building our timetables around the periods which we have been offered.'

2.52   The collaboration between staff in the department and specialist staff was leading to greater specialization in the department. Hazel Coombs, for example, had arrived at the school after the move, and was taking responsibility for science teaching. This meant that she took groups into the science area as well as working on a science curriculum with all those within the department that the staff felt could participate. She was keen to make these real learning experiences rather than 'looking at creepy crawlies under stones again'. When we met she was working on a module on the water cycle.

Participation in lessons

2.53   The way in which Michelle participated in a science lesson, as portrayed in the programme, was not typical of the way students from the special needs department shared in the academic resources of the school. In fact, a year later Michelle no longer joined in science lessons. When we were writing this, shared lessons involved five students from the department, who joined Gwen Woodman's lower-attainment year-10 option groups for English. A number of teachers did envisage greater inclusion within the lessons and not just with bottom sets. But commonly, contact with subject specialists happened when students from the department joined a member of staff in another department who was timetabled to work with them and their teachers.

2.54   Subjects such as music, pottery, sciences, technology (including home economics), PE and games were all taught by mainstream teachers to some pupils from the special needs department. These sessions were prepared jointly when possible. We observed lessons containing rich learning opportunities in which the subject specialism was central to the activity and the teaching strategies and language were adapted to meet the needs of individual students. A group of fifteen-year-olds made clocks in technology; this activity involved planning, measuring,

Pupils enjoy a maths lesson in the special needs department.

Staff at Hirst High share their knowledge and experience in different curriculum areas ...

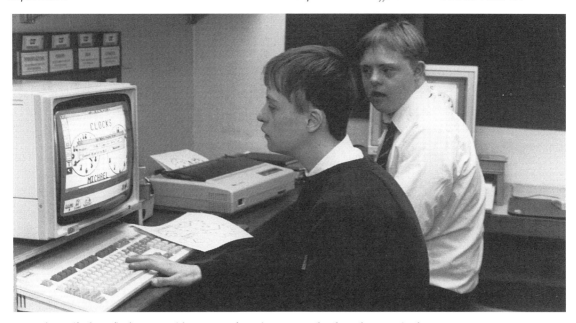
... and pupils benefit from a wide range of equipment and a broader curriculum.

counting, sequencing, painting and using drilling and cutting equipment. It also involved carefully focused discussion on time and time relationships. This was a technology lesson and *Blue Peter* was a thousand miles away. Hazel Coombs had been taking a group to work on forensic science, following a trail of clues in search of missing biscuits. Besides these contacts, a number of students had opted to do work experience or spend their activities week in the special needs department. But it was clear that there was a problem of continuity for some lessons, occurring once every ten-day cycle.

2.55 Janice Trotter involved a group in home economics in a certificate accreditation course. She felt that there was an overlap in attainments between her students from the special needs department and other students, but she was wary of taking groups together:

I've done it in the past and I'm trying to work out how to do it again. At the moment I need all my energies to cope with my mainstream bottom group as a class, and I couldn't face the problem of having extra bodies.

2.56 We discussed the experience of some teachers in other schools, that having students in a group who had obvious needs for support had sometimes been found to reduce rather than exacerbate management problems.

Informal contact between students

2.57 Teachers and learning support staff seemed, in general, to feel enthusiastic about the gains made, largely through informal contact. One teacher commented:

> Their confidence is definitely up a lot because they just walk down the corridors with all the other children and the others speak to them and they'll speak back and that's given them a lot of confidence.

2.58 At the beginning of the day a small group of mainstream pupils met the young people arriving at the special needs department at Hirst High. They helped pupils out of vehicles when needed and accompanied pupils in wheelchairs to their classroom. The entrance to the special needs department was at the side of the building some distance from the main entrance to the school, so pupils of the two communities arrived at the school at the same time, but entered and left through separate doors.

At the start of the school day

Pupils from Hirst High meet those arriving at the special needs department.

Pupils arrive at the same time but enter and leave the school by different doors.

2.59   Dinner time was a pleasant occasion at Hirst High. The atmosphere was calm and friendly. There appeared to be no need to have any formal policing of behaviour, and dinner time was shared by staff, students and local retired people. Those students from the special needs department who were able to eat independently had lunch in the school dining-room. The hall quickly filled up and all pupils, teachers and visitors chose where they sat and mixed well. Those students who required help in eating and most of those who used wheelchairs had their lunch separately in the special needs base.

2.60   The reasons given for this arrangement were:

- the dining room would be too noisy for these pupils;
- their eating difficulties made it inappropriate for them to eat in the main dining hall because it was messy;
- too many wheelchairs would be cumbersome and block passage ways.

2.61   These views were expressed by staff both from mainstream and from the special needs department. You may remember the lunchtime arrangements at the Grove school where all students and staff shared lunchtime, assistance was given to some students with eating, and this was seen as commonplace. Felicity Armstrong reported that, when she was having a cup of tea and toast in the bistro, she noticed a girl from the special needs department aged about sixteen giving a drink and some toast to a partially sighted boy in a wheelchair, with apparently very little expressive language, while she talked to him. She wondered if a time would come in the development of the school when this boy could have had his lunch in the main dining hall with similar help from other students.

2.62   At breaktime in the morning, students and staff in the special needs department ran the 'bistro', where coffee and tea, hot buttered toast and biscuits were served. Some students from outside the department at Hirst High came and joined in, and mixed groups of pupils laughing and talking formed quite naturally. The numbers involved were very small because of the size of the space available and because it was felt that students from outside the department might have taken over if there was an 'open house' policy. Could a school like Hirst High contain a larger coffee bar, somewhere else in the school where all pupils could go?

2.63 At break time and lunchtime, students from the special needs department were kept indoors. Students from the rest of the school had to be outside unless it was raining. It was explained that there was 'nowhere to go' outside for the students from the special needs department. One lunchtime supervisor argued that at the moment there was no-one designated to look after these students outside and that she and the other supervisors already had enough people to look after.

2.64 During the dinner break, pupils from the special needs department were able to go to the youth block. There, students could play table tennis, listen to music and show off their singing talents in the karaoke. Students could also use facilities in the special needs hall which included weight training, snooker, other games and music. By arrangement, particular mainstream students could share this time and there were about six involved in various activities while we were there.

2.65 The kinds of activities that were going on inside and outside the school buildings were things that many teenagers enjoy: hanging around in groups, laughing and talking, listening to music, playing football and other games, looking at books, using the computer and so on. Probably *all* young people enjoy at least one of these activities, they were all available at Hirst High and yet they were not available for all the students to enjoy them together.

Breaktime.

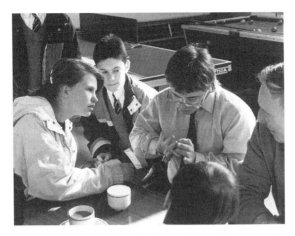

Pupils get together in the bistro for coffee ... and a chat.

A karaoke session takes place in the youth block. Sixth formers from the special needs department sing the latest hits.

Mainstream sixth formers relax in their common area.

Pupils entertain each other in the special needs base.

Physical access

2.66 The design and layout of any institution affects the degree to which those using it can circulate freely and this in turn affects the kinds of social relationships which can develop within it. The new special needs department at Hirst High was part of the main building and close to the office and dining hall. Geographically, it could have been any other department in the school. Its central position could foster contact with the rest of the school.

2.67 However, the department was separated from the rest of the school by large double doors, put in during the renovations, as part of the attempt to give the members of the special needs department 'a secure base'. But students in wheelchairs or with other mobility problems could not go through those doors without assistance, so they were effectively cut off from the rest of the school. Access to the rest of the school was also restricted to the ground floor as there were no lifts. As we have stressed elsewhere in the course, such lack of access affects staff, parents, grandparents and other members of the community as well as students at the school who may or may not be in the special needs department.

2.68 Although there were these drawbacks in the design and layout of the school, other extensive modifications were made to the buildings to make access and participation possible in many areas. In addition to the creation of purpose-built classrooms and speech therapy and physiotherapy rooms, a large entrance hall was built and parts of the school such as the pottery room were altered so that wheelchairs could circulate. But, according to one teacher, the difficulties some students had in moving freely around the school was the biggest problem:

> We are a long way from the classrooms and the double doors prevent many of our students from circulating freely ... The sixth-form block is completely isolated and students have actually

got to go through three double doors to the rest of the block. We have three students in wheelchairs who would be able to get themselves there independently if there were no doors. In the old school, where all the classrooms were arranged around the hall, the students were more independent. Here their independence has gone. They've got to be pushed everywhere and sometimes you need two staff so one can open the doors. The students are aware of that. Debbie, for example, has said, 'I like the new school but I can't get around,' so she's aware that it has put constraints on her.

Contact between staff

2.69   Hirst High was a friendly community and those working there were approachable and helpful. There was a pleasant staffroom, but many department had their own little 'bolt holes' close to their teaching areas where departmental staff tended to meet for a coffee and chat at break time. Those working in large schools will be familiar with the problem of trying to get to the staffroom, drink a cup of coffee and be back in the classroom before the bell rings for the next lesson. This means that all the staff of the school do not meet socially together over coffee, on a daily basis. The staff from the special needs department had their own staffroom in their base and rarely visited the main staffroom.

The attitude of students

2.70   We asked a number of students what they thought about including students from the new special needs department in tutor groups. They *all* thought this was a good idea but there was no school council or similar forum where students and adults could discuss issues and take part in decision-making. Here are a few comments on the inclusion of all students in tutor groups:

> We'd get to know each other and make more friends.

> I think it would be ace. They'd settle in with us lot. They'd have a chance to do what we do.

> I wouldn't mind. We'd get to know them and they'd get to know us. They wouldn't be frightened any more. At the beginning they'd be walking around thinking we might be laughing at them. They wouldn't be so nervous afterwards.

> People would gradually accept. They wouldn't *all* accept straight away. Some would think, 'I don't know what they are doing here.' But they'd just have to get used to it, wouldn't they? I mean, it would be right different if *we* were disabled and had ability problems and that. Then *they'd* have to accept it.

2.71   On the cassette programme we heard Margaret Wells describing the students at Hirst High as 'an incredible population of children who adapt extremely well to all kinds of situations. They are patient and have a lot of humanity.' On the question of shared tutor groups for all pupils, she said:

I think it would work, not so much because of what I think or what the head thinks, or what the special needs department think but because the children of the school have always been the sort of people who would make anything work and I think it would be successful.

The views of parents

2.72 As before other similar moves, parents had been apprehensive. Katy's mother was typical in her positive view of the move once it had taken place.

I was expecting some trauma. I mean, she's a typical seventeen-year-old but with the difficulties of having a disability too. Having been in a fairly sheltered environment for most of her school years I expected the change to have quite a profound effect on her. It has, but in a much more positive way than I expected. I have to say I was very keen for this change, and I was all prepared for more difficult behaviour problems, but no. In fact, in the very short time, I've noticed she's much more mature and much more self-reliant, and her self-esteem has gone up which I think is very important. I think it's due to a lot of things. I think it's the fact that she goes to a school where everybody else goes as well and even the very basic thing of wearing a uniform, she's quite pleased about. In some ways I've always thought uniforms made everybody look too much the same, but it's something they all seem to want to do, and I think the fact that Katy could be seen to be wearing a uniform made her feel, 'Well, I'm wearing one too.' But I think the main reason her self-esteem has gone up is that people talk about schools and she sees where everybody else goes to school. She has always thrived very much on being with other people, with other children and young people who don't necessarily have disabilities.

2.73 This parent talked about the kinds of changes she would like to see take place at Hirst High in the future and the effect the change could have on the expectations of students and parents:

I think Katy would benefit if she could share some lessons with mainstream students in certain areas. Katy's curriculum has got to meet her needs but it's also got to open up other avenues and there are some areas that I would like to see her sharing in that way. It's early days but it is beginning to happen in a very limited way. I would like to see shared break times and shared leisure activities.

I think parents' expectations have always been very limited, they've never thought they should have anything else … they feel 'we should be grateful' and we've been made to feel that way as well. And really, the fact that we've made this step not only are parents' expectations raised but these students' expectations are raised. They'll want more. Not more than anybody else but just the same opportunities.

2.74 Initially information produced by the school for parents tended to omit the concerns of parents with students in the special needs department. But after parents and staff in the department had pointed this out to senior staff, procedures began to be developed to ensure that their perspective was included.

A new role for the special needs department?

2.75 After they joined the school, the staff in the special needs department continued to have responsibility for a particular group of students defined by the statementing process as having 'severe learning difficulties'. There were some indications that this responsibility was beginning to broaden. For example, two distressed homeless students had arrived at the school and, needing particular support, had started life at the school based in the department. (However, when special needs departments become established in schools, there may be a danger that they are seen as taking responsibility for all 'problematic' students and this may reduce the involvement of other members of staff.) The skills that department staff had to offer students across the school in a variety of curriculum areas were also recognized. There was a suggestion that learning support as a whole could be seen as emanating from the department and that this could come to define a new broader role in the school. As Gwen Woodman acknowledged in response to this suggestion:

> We're at the middle stage of where do we go now, of getting that right, of moving on from here. That isn't pie in the sky though, why shouldn't that be the learning support department? That would be wonderful. That would seem to me some kind of ultimate goal that they should be seen as the people that help to support every child in the school who has difficulties at the start, and then go on from there.

Including some, excluding others?

2.76 The presence in the school of some students who had statements prompts questions about the absence of others. When the programme was being made, there was a practice of sending students who were perceived as being more able than the students in the special needs department but who were categorized as having 'moderate learning difficulties' to a special school in Morpeth. It would be hard to provide a legal defence of that practice if parents appealed against it, given the provision available in the mainstream at Hirst High and at the middle and first school. But the head was wary that if increasing numbers of students perceived as having difficulties attended the school this might affect the image of the school as concerned with achievement.

2.77 And what of other disabled students? Could the school support students who are physically disabled or are deaf? Could it have a policy of including all students within its communities, irrespective of attainment or disability?

Activity 4   How could participation be enhanced? ─────────

Make a list of what could be done to facilitate the participation of the students and staff of the special needs department in the rest of the school. Then take one item on your list and devise a strategy for implementing the change.

2.78   Below are a number of questions you might have considered although you may well be able to think of many other issues:

- Could students share the same school entrances?

- Could students share break times?

- Could there be more informal meeting areas like the bistro for all students?

- Could more staff share staffrooms?

- Could all students share tutor groups?

- Could students share lessons more frequently?

- Could lifts be installed?

- Could physical circulation of students be eased?

- What joint in-service training might be arranged?

- Could the special needs department be combined with learning support into a single learning support department?

CONCLUSION: RAISING QUESTIONS

2.79   As one way of documenting the response of Hirst High to the diversity of its students we examined the way students were divided into groups on the basis of their attainments and presumed ability. We stumbled on a by-product of this classification system in the dramatic gender imbalance within attainment sets. This imbalance was only one consequence of attempting to implement contradictory aims within this as in other schools. At Hirst High staff wish to value the achievement of students but also to divide them on this basis. This section has provided an examination of the way these pressures were interacting in one school.

2.80   The study of grouping, as well as of the timetabling policies, helped us to make sense of the possibilities for, and progress in, the inclusion of students from Riverbank Special School. Hirst High School was in the very early stages of developing a whole school community from two different populations of staff and students. Already, great changes had taken place in the lives of the relatively small number of students and the staff who had come from Riverbank school. The changes for the large number of students and staff who were already at the school had been fewer, so far. How would you like to see the school develop?

'Sir, we won two nil!'

3 CONTROLLING CHANGE

3.1 The teachers at Hirst High were attempting to control the way their school developed while outside pressures forced their hands. In particular, they faced cuts in their budget and rising unemployment in their area. They were also in the throes of introducing the National Curriculum and responding to the pressure to be competitive resulting from the 1988 Education Act. In this section we will consider further pressures on and opportunities for schools after the 1993 Education Act. We will then look at the process of creating a formal school development plan as one way for teachers to give priority to their own principles while accommodating legislation which may be designed according to others'. We then analyse the views of some people working in special schools with a range of visions of the future. We provide two examples of changes to special schools which were instigated by their own staff and supported by LEAs.

PICKING UP THE 1992 EDUCATION BILL

3.2 After the vast changes to the education system introduced by the 1988 Education Act, very few people anticipated that a new education bill would reach Parliament in 1992 that would break the record for the bill with the largest number of clauses in educational history. Its central purpose was to boost the number of schools opting out of local authority control, which by 11 January 1993 numbered 655 in England and Wales, with a majority in areas with Conservative local councils (Association of Metropolitan Authorities, 1993, briefing paper for MPs). But it also established a new framework for supporting these schools through regionalized funding agencies appointed by central government, and for setting up 'education associations' to devise plans to improve 'failing schools' in readiness for them being taken into the grant-maintained sector.

3.3 Apart from the official opposition in Parliament and from the teachers and their professional associations, the bill met with an unusual degree of opposition from normally loyal Conservative supporters. County councillors objected to the further erosion of their powers and were even joined by the Conservative chair of the Parliamentary Select Committee on Education, Sir Malcolm Thornton, who suggested that the proposed changes to the education system were a 'recipe for at best confusion and at worst chaos'. He argued that think tanks such as the Centre for Policy Studies had had undue negative influence: 'Sadly whole sections of our nation once respected for common sense have been brainwashed into an acceptance of their dogma' (*The Times Educational Supplement*, 4 December 1992).

3.4 The main elements of the bill are summarized in Figure 1. The Secretary of State envisaged that the significance of education authorities would be so reduced after the act that there would be no necessity for local authorities to retain education committees. They were to retain responsibility for 'special needs' education but, according to an article in *Education*, some civil servants in the DfE, fearing the demise of large sections of their functions, suspected that special needs would be hived off eventually to local government social services committees and handled at central government level by the Department of Health and Social Security (*Education*, 6 November 1992, p. 362). This fear contrasted with the positive role prescribed for LEAs by the Audit Commission/ HMI report, *Getting the Act Together* (Audit Commission/HMI, 1992b). Drawing on practice in a variety of LEAs, including the Children First Policy in Nottinghamshire examined in Unit 15, the authors of this report saw a role for LEAs as contributors to and co-ordinators of 'special needs' policy and as 'champions of children with special needs'. This report was virtually the last act of an independent HMI before they became part of a new quango, the Office for Standards in Education, or OFSTED.

Figure 1 *The main elements of the 1992–3 Education Bill* (The Times Educational Supplement, *6 November 1992, p. 14).*

3.5 The bill proposed a number of minor modifications to the 1981 Education Act which it would incorporate and replace. The principal changes would be in the composition and powers of 'tribunals' set up to deal with appeals in relation to the statementing process. It was envisaged that these would be chaired by qualified lawyers rather than local councillors, as at present. They would gain a certain degree of impartiality but would cost considerably more. At present appeals committees have the power only to reject the appeal or to recommend to LEAs that the statement be reconsidered (which LEAs can ignore). The decisions of the new tribunals would be binding on LEAs and they would have powers to vary the content of statements.

3.6 The bill responded to national concern about exclusions by proposing that LEAs and the funding agency be given powers to compel local authority or grant-maintained schools to take excluded students. This contrasts with the DfE's suggestion in its discussion paper on exclusions issued at the end of 1992 that schools which excluded students would be financially penalized and schools which took in students from another school would be financially rewarded (DfE, 1992b). This discussion paper included the results of the government survey of permanent exclusions discussed in Unit 11/12. Returns for this survey were provided voluntarily by LEAs. The results supported other findings about the overwhelming preponderance of boys and the over-representation of Afro-Caribbean students. Very few cases of permanent exclusion were for violence against staff. During the passage of the bill, however, a new social panic arose over juvenile crime, brought to a head by the death of a small boy abducted by two older boys. Following this, the government proposed an amendment to the bill requiring LEAs to establish new forms of provision for excluded pupils. They were thus proposing two opposing strategies, those of getting excluded pupils back into the mainstream and of providing them with segregated education. As suggested in Unit 11/12, such segregated provision may draw even more students out of the mainstream (see Reader 2, Chapter 29).

3.7 While it is always possible that a bill can be transformed in Parliament, in early 1993 it seemed unlikely that any major changes would be made to this one. At its Commons committee stage, a committee of seventeen Conservative MPs, fifteen Labour MPs and one SLD MP went through the bill clause by clause and proposed amendments. Small constructive changes are occasionally accepted, such as the suggestion that governors must be warned before an item appears on their agenda discussing opting out. However, the built-in majority meant that voting for each clause was routine unless the Parliamentary Under Secretary of State for Schools, Eric Forth (orchestrating the progress of the bill because the Secretary of State John Pattern decided not to attend this stage), chose to accept a particular amendment or propose a compromise.

FORMAL SCHOOL PLANS

3.8 Increasingly, as we are indicating here, and as was argued in Units 14 and 15, the responsibility for the detailed planning of education change is being removed from LEAs. But from whatever direction outside pressures come, it has always been important for those working in schools who wish to retain a sense of ownership over their destinies to devise their own plans for development. In the case of Hirst High we saw that the suggestions from some teachers that a formal, agreed, explicit plan for incorporating ex-Riverbank students into the heart of school life was not supported by management. What difference would such a plan make to a school?

Activity 5   Planning school development

Christine Gilbert, the deputy director of education in the London Borough of Harrow, was formerly head of Whitmore School which was described and discussed in Unit 1/2. She has written a chapter for us on school development plans called 'Planning school development', which is Chapter 3 in Reader 2. A development plan for Whitmore High School is used as an example in that chapter. It is a detailed chapter, with some education jargon, and how much you want to go into its details may depend on your position within education. At the most general level, when you have read it you should have a reasonably clear idea about how you would set about co-ordinating a development plan for a primary or secondary school, either of which may be a special school, and perhaps be able to think how the principles might be applied to a nursery school or further education college. It may help you to consider the following questions as you read the chapter.

- How would you convince a group of staff that a formal development plan was a good idea?

- What stages would you go through when drawing up a plan?

- Who would you involve?

- How would you determine the priorities for the short and long term?

3.9   We do not intend to repeat the detail of the chapter here but to emphasize two points. It is striking how the complexity of the planning process increases with the size of the school and in secondary rather than primary schools. Any shared development plan for a further education college or a university would be extremely difficult to achieve. Christine Gilbert also stresses that the process of producing the plan is as important as its content:

> ... joint ownership of the plan not only gives the school a clearer and more united sense of purpose, but also reduces the stress generated by the speed and extent of educational changes.
>
> (Reader 2, p. 69)

PERSPECTIVES FROM SPECIAL SCHOOLS

3.10   We do not need to remind you that the writers of this course have not taken a neutral line about the inclusion of students who experience difficulties or have disabilities within the mainstream. We set out our aims in the *Course Guide* and two of the aims specifically encourage the process of integration:

- To enable students to facilitate a process of increasing the inclusion and participation of pupils from special schools and separate units within mainstream groups.

- To encourage the development of teaching methods and curricula which support the shared learning of diverse groups.

(*Course Guide*, p. 5)

3.11   Because of our aims and the principles that underlie them, there has been an emphasis on examples of mainstream practice in the course and we know that at some points this has left some of you feeling less than fully included. We want you all to feel valued as learners, but does the emphasis on mainstream schools and colleges mean that the work of some course participants is devalued? That is not our intention. We know that there are excellent staff and excellent lessons in special schools. But we would not wish to slide out of controversy by coming up with the often repeated diplomatic formula that 'special schools do an excellent job and there will always be a place for them'. This leaves open the question of how big the segregated sector should be, and whether it should be greater or smaller than it is at present. Nor would we wish to encourage the simplistic opinion that all or most of those working in special schools oppose integration. As will be clear from this unit and elsewhere in the course many of the most imaginative and forceful ideas about integration have emerged from special schools. If we are true to our principles then we have to spell out that we would like to see very few students educated outside the mainstream. An appropriately resourced and supported mainstream would include virtually all those at present in special schools. This is not an idealistic option but a logical consequence of examining real possibilities for the inclusion of students in the mainstream.

3.12   The examples provided in this unit, in addition to those elsewhere in the course, should help you to reflect on the extent to which you agree with us. We think that it is not sensible to attempt to run both an integrated and segregated system with the distribution to be determined by choices of parents and students and the vagaries of professional opinion, partly because to run two systems is an expensive option. We argue that where the reallocation of resources is carefully planned, an integrated system need be no more expensive than one relying on the continuation of special schools (see Audit Commission/HMI, 1992a). Students at the Grove School were supported, for example, with resource reallocated from the special school budget. In moving from one system to the other, however, there are start-up costs, for example in adapting buildings and duplicating staff and resources (see Coopers and Lybrand, 1992). But the main reason for making a policy choice is that the principles underlying the two systems send incompatible messages to mainstream schools. The maintenance of a selective approach undermines an inclusive one. But where special schools do remain there can be little justification for continuing with compulsory segregation. Would special schools survive if parents could not be compelled to send their students there and could expect to gain the same level of resource to support their children within the mainstream?

3.13   At an E242 day school in Cambridge, some students opened a discussion about how these issues were considered within the course. With one student, Jo Koegel, who is deaf and works with young people who are deaf and blind, this discussion continued by fax. She was doing E242 as part of an advanced diploma in health and social welfare, having already studied the *Issues of Deafness* course. Another student, Sally Davies, who works in a school for students categorized as having 'moderate learning difficulties', set down her concerns in a letter. She wrote when she had finished Unit 8/9 and perhaps her thoughts would have been different if she had read further units. She felt at the time that the course undervalued the contribution of special school staff to the education of young people. Here is her letter:

> In the *Course Guide* for E242 *Learning for All* one of the stated aims is:
>
>> To enable students to understand the system of education and special education.
>
> In order to do this I feel that students must be presented with a clear, balanced view of what exists at the present time in the world of special education. An explanation of the variety of schools would be appropriate. Whilst many students may be aware of schools that cater for physical or mental disabilities, are they also aware of the schools which are termed MLD or EBD? Are they aware of the role that these schools play or is the course presenting them as devalued aspects of education? The course materials have made references to such schools – Unit 6/7's descriptions of mathematical activities and a collaborative learning project, for example, both serve to illustrate styles of teaching which are normal practice in special schools but this is not necessarily the impression given.
>
> Throughout the course materials there is a great emphasis on integration of pupils who experience difficulties or have disabilities and on methods by which successful integration can be achieved. Where in this course are students told about the success and achievements made in MLD and EBD schools? These schools also have 'values' in education and are acutely aware of the need for socialization and emotional as well as physical development. Indeed it is often these schools which are better able to adapt circumstances to allow and promote such development in a way which is more

structured towards the needs of the particular child and which is less threatening than the approach and atmosphere to which some pupils are exposed in some examples of integration. Not all segregation is a failure and not all integration is a success.

The course places integration in direct opposition to segregation, seeing it as the only solution to the problem of creating an education system that is open and fair to all. To integrate pupils in mainstream schools does not necessarily mean greater achievement, adjustment or equality. It is very difficult to make it work, it is not a cheap option and it is fraught with political problems. Will the course discuss or make allowance for the financial and political decisions which are not made by teachers?

Finally, if students following this course are to be given the opportunity to reflect on the impact of the National Curriculum on children who experience difficulties, does Will Swann's chapter 'Hardening the hierarchies' [Reader 1, Chapter 7] provide a balanced view? Whilst I would agree that not everything about the NC is perfect I feel that it has opened up new opportunities for curriculum discussion and the sharing of resources between schools not just between special and mainstream schools but also between infant, junior, primary and secondary phases.

If E242 *Learning for All* is to mean 'all', then I feel that the course must examine educational practice as it exists today. Integration is one aspect of this practice and segregation is another. One of the other tasks should be how to make both valued elements of the system and not to promote prejudice or disaffection and certainly not to promote the one at the expense of the valuable and principled work done by the other.

Sally Davies

3.14   Tony Booth introduced the categories of special school in Unit 1/2, page 50, paragraphs 3.76 to 3.78. He hopes that he didn't confuse anyone by the reference to ESN(M) schools on page 47 which changed their designation in the early 1980s. He was referring to past referral processes and meant to say 'in what were then referred to provocatively as Educationally Subnormal (Moderate) [ESN(M)] schools'. These are now usually referred to as 'moderate learning difficulties' schools. The provision for students categorized as having 'emotional and behavioural difficulties' is discussed in Unit 11/12. However, it is true that nowhere in the course is there as detailed a picture of what goes on inside a special school as those of the Grove or Whitmore in Unit 1/2 or Hirst High in the previous section of this unit, although Tim Southgate does redress the balance later in this section.

3.15   We think that good teaching occurs in a wide variety of places, inside and outside schools. Sally Davies feels that teachers in special schools may be especially adept at responding to the particular needs of individuals and providing a 'less threatening' atmosphere. We argue that you can find responsive teachers and confident students, who have

40

experienced difficulties in learning, within mainstream and special schools. We also point to the contradiction in special schools grouping students according to categories of disability or inability and then attempting to respond to them 'as individuals'. Sally Davies seems to believe that we are suggesting that 'all segregation is a failure' and 'all integration is a success'. We do not see it in those terms. We feel that each of us needs to come to a carefully considered view about the system of education we would prefer, recognizing that any human system will have its share of success and failure. The view we have come to, is that a system which works towards inclusion and participation and against exclusion is to be preferred to one in which present levels of exclusion are encouraged or increased. Sally Davies feels that we should not promote one approach 'at the expense of the valuable and principled work done by the other'. We argue that it would be dishonest not to follow through the clear implications of our principles and the aims for this course.

3.16   Sally Davies also makes a point about Will Swann's view of the National Curriculum and the positive effect she feels that the National Curriculum has had on broadening discussion of the curriculum and on the sharing of resources. We recognize the positive effects that national curriculum discussions have made to the breadth of the curriculum. In raising the spectre of exemptions, it has brought out into the open, too, a shared view within mainstream and special schools that all students have an entitlement to broad curricular opportunities.

Activity 6   Changing places

Chapter 4 in Reader 2 is about the developments that have taken place in a special school in Oxford and the way it supports its students. It is written by the head teacher, Tim Southgate, who became an enthusiastic supporter of integration for most disabled students and of separate conductive education for some. Many of the issues it raises were brought to your attention in previous units, particularly Units 1/2, 8/9 and Unit 10. As you read the chapter you might consider the following questions:

- What was the rationale for grouping disabled students together at Ormerod School in the early 1980s?

- How was integration based on the needs of students?

- How important for the successful participation of disabled students was the statement of principles by the head teacher of Marlborough Comprehensive School?

- To what extent do you agree with the idea of grouping students together for conductive education in a community separated from the mainstream?

3.17 The chapter describes the way Tim Southgate and the Ormerod staff collaborated with mainstream schools to promote the integration of students. Oxfordshire allowed individual schools the autonomy to develop in this way before local management of schools, and Ormerod was sufficiently well resourced to initiate the necessary adaptations to buildings. Bureaucratic hurdles were minimal. The changes in the school fitted into a local authority policy encouraging integration, though not in a highly co-ordinated fashion (see Jones, 1983; Sayer, 1987; CSIE, 1992).

3.18 When Tim Southgate became head teacher of Ormerod he inherited a special school which contained students sent there because of physical disability. It might seem that there was an educational principle, albeit a mistaken one, underlying such a practice; that students with a category of disability in common were seen to require common curricula or teaching methods. However, as Tim Southgate explains, in schools for students categorized by disability, there may be a wider range of attainment and interest than is found in most mainstream schools. The classification is medical and administrative rather than educational.

3.19 Tim Southgate argues that:

> The school has been led throughout by the needs of the children and as these needs have changed or the perception or understanding of them has altered so the school has responded by creating new structures and developing new approaches.

But according to Tim Southgate himself, Ormerod School was set up to cater for a category of disability rather than the educational needs of its students. And if it was not set up according to 'need', could it be dismantled according to 'need'? A pragmatic response to the circumstances he inherited seems to be represented here as being 'led throughout by the needs of the children'.

3.20 The concept of need is problematic, in itself, as was pointed out at the start of the course. The needs of students are usually defined in terms of other people's perceptions. This further reduces the force of Tim Southgate's concern that integration should be seen as a response to need, rather than as a human right or 'an end in itself'. We are not sure what seeing integration 'as an end in itself' means. We suspect that he is arguing that an integrated system is not to be preferred to a segregated one on moral grounds as good, or preferable 'in itself'. He differs then from the writers of this course who argue that an inclusive system in which the diversity of students is celebrated and students learn co-operatively together irrespective of their attainments or disabilities, is morally desirable. Equally we argue that a comprehensive, community-oriented system of nursery, primary and secondary schools and ultimately and ideally further and higher education, is to be preferred to a system selecting by attainment, disability or wealth. This preference is based on a view of the society we would like for ourselves and our children. It makes little sense to suggest that a comprehensive and selective system should exist in parallel or even less that the choice between the systems can be based on need. Although we argue for this

42

system this does not mean that we demand that others share our perspective. We ask only that others analyse the moral or social principles as well as the pragmatic and practical considerations which underlay their choices.

3.21   Do children and young people have a *right* to attend a mainstream school or their local school? Do parents have a *right* to be able to send them to one? We would argue that students do have the right to attend their local school but that this right may conflict in extreme cases with the rights of others to learn or work free from intimidation or violence. Unit 11/12 looked at issues of control and disaffection and you will be aware of the complexity of the causes of disruption in schools and what can be done to minimize it. People also have the right to form groups based on culture, identity and interest. But Tim Southgate does not make a distinction between such voluntary separation and the compulsory segregation that can be an outcome of the statementing process. *We see compulsory segregation as an infringement of human rights.*

3.22   Gerry O'Hagan, who was head of Marlborough school when students from Ormerod started moving there, did not think that his school had 'a right to refuse any child from [the] catchment area if the parent wanted the child to attend' (Reader 2, p. 73). Although Tim Southgate does not recognize this right he seemed to regard the principle as of great significance in easing the process of inclusion of his students. Of course, people can state one set of principles while basing their practice on another set entirely. It is actions and the often implicit principles which underlie them which are more important than rhetoric. In the case of Marlborough school, it seems that the principles were stated *and* acted upon.

3.23   Marlborough was not the local school for many of the disabled students and the Ormerod staff showed an unusual degree of flexibility in starting and adapting schemes so that more students could attend their neighbourhood schools. This local initiative was able to create a more sophisticated model of integration than common in many LEAs, where advisers may act as if the task of promoting integration is over once a mainstream school has been resourced to include a group of students from a special school.

3.24   The Ormerod model conformed more closely to our view of integration as a never-ending process of increasing the participation of students in the educational and social life of mainstream schools and communities. When thought of in this way, integration can be seen to involve all students and merge with the ideals of comprehensive, community, lifelong education. Integration, like democracy, can be seen to involve an unending series of steps bringing people greater knowledge and control of the decisions and social practices which affect their lives. This is a further meaning that can be given to rejecting integration as 'an end in itself'.

3.25   But the idea of links for students between special and mainstream schools have sometimes been put into practice as if any contact must be good 'in itself'. Thus at one special school at which Tony Booth was a governor, a particular student was attending four mainstream schools 'for integration' as well as his special school. In his governor's report, Tony Booth suggested that given the incredible flexibility that was expected of this student in adapting to five schools perhaps he should go to only one mainstream school, but attend it full-time.

3.26   Ormerod transmuted, finally, into a school for students with a narrower range of ages and disabilities who followed a curriculum based on conductive education. The numbers were back up to the levels of the early 1980s. Given the narrowed range, some of these students must have travelled even greater distances than those who had attended the special school, previously. The arguments surrounding conductive education were considered in Unit 8/9 and we will not repeat them here. But if the special school had not already been in existence, would we have set up a conductive education group away from the mainstream?

Activity 7   Moving on, moving in and moving out

Even greater changes were taking place at another special school in Oxfordshire in the 1980s. Roger Kidd, then head of Bishopswood School for students categorized as having severe learning difficulties, worked with his staff and collaborating mainstream schools, with support from the LEA, to transfer the children and young people from his school into the mainstream. Brief details of this process were considered in the previous section. He left the school to take up a post as head of Etton Pasture Special School for students categorized as having 'moderate learning difficulties' in the East Riding area of Humberside, and repeated the Bishopswood formula over a four-year period there. Chapter 5 in Reader 2 is his description of the way the students and resources were transferred from his school into the mainstream. As you read the chapter you might consider the following issues:

- To what extent are the approaches to change developed within one LEA relevant to a different one?

- What justifications are there for maintaining special schools for students categorized as having moderate learning difficulties?

- To what extent would you wish to include approaches to difficulties in learning and behaviour within a single policy?

- What are the advantages and disadvantages of basing a learning support service within the special education sector of an LEA rather than in particular schools?

3.27   When Roger Kidd moved to Humberside he found that initially he had less scope for contributing to changes in policy than he had had in Oxfordshire. However, the preparation of an LEA-wide strategy meant that, overall, the reduction of segregation might be more far-reaching.

There was a clear recognition within the plan that integration was a continuing process that did not stop once students were attached to a resource base within a mainstream school.

3.28 Roger Kidd had been convinced by his experience at Bishopswood school that if students categorized as having severe learning difficulties could be in the mainstream then there could be no justification for excluding students said to have moderate learning difficulties. He was determined that they should receive the same level of support within the mainstream as they received in Etton Pasture. Continuity of support was assured when he became head of the East Riding support service.

3.29 However, the education of students who had acquired the label of having 'emotional and behavioural difficulties' was not part of the LEA integration plan. When Etton Pasture closed, it reopened as a redesignated special school and five of the teachers opted to stay on. The new school allowed some students to be educated within Humberside who had previously been sent out to residential provision. However, given the pressures in the 1990s to exclude students seen to be difficult in behaviour that were documented in Unit 11/12, it is likely that the filling of one special school will do little to relieve them. An opportunity was lost, perhaps temporarily, to bring together policies about difficulties in learning and behaviour. Given that inappropriate curricula can lead to disaffection and disruption, then it is always possible that students coming out of the special school they had attended because of experiencing learning difficulties in the mainstream might return there under a new title of having 'emotional and behavioural difficulties'. A growing segregated sector for students said to have emotional and behavioural difficulties is a discouragement to schools to make connections between difficulties in learning, behaviour and control.

3.30 Humberside has gone down the route of developing a large support service, funded by the LEA special education budget, with some staff based in mainstream and others working peripatetically. Such services are vulnerable to cuts, particularly since models of funding are now based on individual mainstream or special schools. These problems were discussed in Unit 15, particularly in relation to Staffordshire learning support service (see Chapter 34 in Reader 2). In the absence of very clear and effective co-ordinating powers over special education outside and within the mainstream, LEAs are caught between two alternatives. Do they retain support teachers and hope that schools will pay for them or do they devolve them to schools and hope that schools will continue to give students who experience difficulties a sufficient degree of priority?

4 A COMMON CONCERN

4.1   The course has covered a wide area and some students have written to us or told us that they would have liked greater concentration on particular topics. But this broad area also creates problems of definition. What do all the areas of study that we have placed together have in common? What unites discussion of policies for the under-fives in Unit 5, of truancy in Unit 10/11, of power and influence in education in Unit 14, and of the language of instruction in producing and preventing difficulties in learning in Unit 6/7? After all, the concerns of the course seem to cover the whole of education rather than a small segment of it.

4.2   We have a number of connected ideas for drawing our field of study together. We share a common concern to reduce or prevent the difficulties, of learning or participation, that children and young people experience in education. *We see the project of this course as a shared attempt to describe and understand the education system from the perspective of students who experience difficulties or experience exclusion from full participation in the educational and social life of mainstream schools and colleges.* It is a position of understanding of, or advocacy for, or alliance with, students who experience difficulties or devaluation or have disabilities. It is our method for beginning to reduce the difficulties faced by students.

4.3   In attempting to make sense of the world of education from the perspective of those who have difficulties in it, in trying to remove barriers to learning and participation, we develop a critique of education. We argue that this critique is valuable for the whole of the education system since it is concerned with the development of an approach to education that is appropriate for all students. At the heart of this critique is a view of the relationship between students, curricula and education staff.

4.4   Does a shared interest in reducing the difficulties students encounter commit us to a common set of principles to inform our practice? In his survey of mainstream 'special needs' practice, Alan Dyson (1992) has distinguished between 'state of the art' good practice in schools and 'innovatory practice' which is said to be at the cutting edge of transformations of learning support and development. The notions of 'good practice' or 'state of the art practice' or 'innovatory practice' presume a common purpose. Yet what is good or innovatory for some, may be anathema to others. In 1992 Goebbels' diaries were serialized in the *Sunday Times*. The innovatory solution to diversity associated with Goebbels is not part of what most of us would regard as good practice. What other practices does our common concern exclude?

4.5   At various points in the course, we have discussed two opposing solutions to teaching the diversity of students in schools which can be called 'selective' and 'inclusive'. Each is informed by a set of moral and political values which in turn limits the approaches to reducing difficulties in schools, to raising standards. The selective approach starts from the assumption that learning takes place best in groups of 'similar' learners and involves a search for ways of selecting and matching students, methods, curricula and schools. It assumes further that the process and prospect of selection provide incentives to try harder and disincentives to falling behind.

4.6   We have argued that selection and segregation are inevitably bound up with the ascription of differences in worth to students on the basis of background, attainment and disability. The devaluation of students creates a pool of potential disaffection which contributes to difficulties in learning. If it contributes to devaluation and difficulties in learning, the selective approach conflicts with our common concern. And for this reason the selective solution to raising standards in schools may be self-defeating.

4.7   But we have to recognize that practice is often informed by a mass of conflicting principles emerging from ourselves or others with authority over us, which push in opposing directions. For example, rigid setting arrangements may be created alongside an attempt to value the diversity of backgrounds and attainments of all students. Such opposing forces were evident at Hirst High School. However, it seems to surprise some people that practices should be chosen because of principle. For example, Trevor Payne has questioned the preoccupation with in-class support rather than withdrawal in the following way:

> With very few exceptions, readers and audiences were exhorted to embrace the concept of in-class support for children with learning difficulties as a *fait accompli*, as an almost moral and social imperative. Those teachers still daring to actually withdraw children from their mainstream classes for 'remedial tuition' (both unfashionable words) must have felt like accomplices to some form of educational apartheid.
>
> (Payne, 1992, p. 61)

4.8   As we have argued in Units 1/2 and 6/7, Trevor Payne is right in drawing attention to a real problem. Some teachers do avoid withdrawal because they think it is frowned upon. But he misunderstands the source of the difficulty. It usually arises because the relationship between principles and practices is left unstated. In-class support is promoted, at least in part, because when used effectively it can help to promote inclusive classroom strategies for differentiating curricula. Withdrawal is rejected as a general solution to resolving difficulties in learning because it helps to support the myth of homogeneity; that most students require the same approach and content in their lessons, which in turn promotes inflexible teaching.

4.9   It is clear that the circumstances in which principles are applied change dramatically. Central and local government policies and changes in the level of resources create a kaleidoscope of shifting contexts. In several areas at the moment cuts in local budgets have led to the threat of the sudden withdrawal of support for some students in the mainstream. In other areas mainstream support has never materialized and parents are asking LEAs to provide special school placements as a result (*Guardian Education*, 16 March 1993, p. 2). There are daily pronouncements about changes in the National Curriculum or testing arrangements or union opposition to tests. The strains of introducing a secondary-led subject-based National Curriculum are being felt, particularly in some primary schools, and the 'mental health' of head teachers is said to have deteriorated (*The Times Educational Supplement*, 19 March 1993, p. 4). A shift to more subject-based teaching in classes divided by attainment has been urged for primary schools and the provision of different standard attainment tasks for students according to curriculum level is pushing those secondary schools which have retained mixed-ability groups to move towards a greater use of sets (*The Times Educational Supplement*, 19 March 1993, p. 5). On a positive note, the Office for Standards in Education argued that standards of lessons had risen in English, science and, with qualification, in maths, though they had fallen in technology (*The Times Educational Supplement*, 19 March 1993, p. 4).

4.10   Priorities about which difficulties should receive our attention change. New priorities may be a product of changing policies or may force themselves on us through media and other social pressures. As priorities change it is inevitable that the work of those in the system who concern themselves with difficulties in schools will also change. Unit 1/2 refers to the (as yet) small number of children in the UK who are infected with HIV or are affected by having a family member with HIV or AIDS. Unit 11/12 documents a growing concern with bullying and sexual and racial harassment.

4.11   Change which should have taken place in some areas of practice has been limited. The rigid demarcation which still exists in some schools between those who are meant to respond to difficulties of behaviour and control and those who busy themselves with supporting learning makes little theoretical or practical sense. The major impact teachers can make in reducing disaffection in schools is through the curriculum, just as it is for preventing and reducing difficulties in learning.

4.12   We have still a long way to go, too, before there is an acceptance of diversity in the sexual orientation of students. About ten per cent of young people grow up as gay or lesbian. They often feel a sense of exclusion which may interfere with learning in school. We think that we should accept and value the diversity of students as good in itself, not because it may raise attainment levels. But showing how the devaluation of or low expectations for students can lead to disaffection and underachievement provides an added reason to place the valuing of diversity at the centre of our common concern.

CONCLUDING REMARKS

4.13 In this course we have argued that a clear and explicit set of principles should inform an approach to diversity in schools. Differences in principle may lead to conflict but the belief that education changes through consensus is false. It enables those with power to reduce opposition to their policies. The reaction of some to the illusion of consultation before the 1988 Education Act or the 1993 Education Act, can be likened to a Thurber cartoon. It depicts two fencers. One of them cries 'Touché!' as he swings and cuts off the head of the other. There is a look of affront and recrimination in the eyes of the severed head at this breach of etiquette. But it is too late.

Touché!

4.14 However, there are signs that the movement towards more selective and competitive schools, which promote failure as a necessary side-effect of success, may falter in the long term. The rise in the numbers of temporary and permanent exclusions may yet point to a politically unacceptable end result of selective policies within schools. But a main cause for our optimism is that people do not want their local school to become extinct in the struggle for survival. Most parents and students want a good neighbourhood school. For the writers of this course, a good local school is one that serves and values all the members of its communities.

4.15   We have chosen to end the course, as we started it with an image of an assembly. In November 1992, Dorothy Bordass, who created the lithograph of Midsummer Fair that serves as the cover image of celebration and inclusion for this course, died, aged 85. It seemed appropriate to finish the course with her image of a theatre audience. For us it symbolizes an assembly of diversity.

REFERENCES

AUDIT COMMISSION/HMI (1992a) *Getting in on the Act: provision for pupils with special educational needs*, London, HMSO.

AUDIT COMMISSION/HMI (1992b) *Getting the Act Together: a management handbook for schools and local education authorities*, London, HMSO.

BOOTH, T. and JONES, A. (1987) 'Extending primary practice' in BOOTH, T, POTTS, P. and SWANN, W. (eds) *Curricula for All: preventing difficulties in learning*, Oxford, Blackwell/The Open University.

CENTRE FOR STUDIES OF INTEGRATION IN EDUCATION (CSIE) (1992) *Bishopswood: good practice transferred*, London, HMSO.

COOPERS AND LYBRAND (1992) *Within Reach: access for disabled children to mainstream education*, London, the National Union of Teachers and the Spastics Society.

DEPARTMENT FOR EDUCATION (DFE) (1992a) *Choice and Diversity: a new framework for schools*, London, HMSO.

DEPARTMENT FOR EDUCATION (DFE) (1992b) *Exclusions: a discussion paper*, London, HMSO.

DYSON, A. (1992) 'Innovatory mainstream practice: what's happening in schools' provision for special needs?', *Support for Learning*, **7**(2), pp. 51–57

JONES, N. (1983) 'The management of integration: the Oxfordshire experience' in Booth, T. and Potts, P. (eds) *Integrating Special Education*, Oxford, Blackwell/The Open University.

JUPP, K. (1992) *Everyone Belongs: mainstream education for children with severe learning difficulties*, London, Souvenir Press.

PAYNE, T. (1992) 'It's cold in the other room', *Support for learning*, **6**(2), pp. 61–5

SAYER, J. (1987) 'Secondary schools as a resource for everyone's learning' in BOOTH, T. and POTTS, P. (eds) *Integrating Special Education*, Oxford, Blackwell/The Open University.

ACKNOWLEDGEMENTS

Cartoon

'Touché' from 'The Lady on the Bookcase' from *The Beast in Me and Other Animals* by James Thurber (Hamish Hamilton, 1949). Copyright © James Thurber, 1949. Reproduced by permission of Hamish Hamilton Ltd and Rosemary Thurber.

E242: UNIT TITLES

Unit 1/2   Making Connections

Unit 3/4   Learning from Experience

Unit 5   Right from the Start

Unit 6/7   Classroom Diversity

Unit 8/9   Difference and Distinction

Unit 10   Reading Critically

Unit 11/12   Happy Memories

Unit 13   Further and Higher

Unit 14   Power in the System

Unit 15   Local Authority?

Unit 16   Learning for All